MW01680995

Student Ministry Volunteers Pocket Guide

Best Practices for Leading Your Volunteers

Linda Oliver

Reformed Youth Ministries

rym publishing

Reformed Youth Ministries

7350 Jefferson Highway

Ste 485 PMB 231

Baton Rouge, LA 70806

www.rym.org

RYM Publishing is a division of Reformed Youth Ministries, a ministry that exists to serve the church in their efforts to reach and equip youth for Christ.

Written by Linda Oliver

Edited by John Perritt

Cover design by Joey Kime

ISBN 979-8-9906983-1-4 (print)

ISBN 979-8-9906983-3-8 (digital)

Contents

Acknowledgments

Many youth workers contributed ideas to this resource. Thank you to Adam Brokaw, Austin Lenox, Bobby Epps, Chris Bond, Chrishon Ducker, Gianna Rakes, Jake Allen, Jason Kriaski, Joey Perez, John Spencer, Joshua Holestine, Justin Knowles, Kyle Hoffsmith, Lynne Howard, Mary Katherine Keel, Matt Beham, Michelle Hamilton, Scott Byrd, Scott Herron, Sonny Walker, Stephen Smith, Travis Chapman, Tree Triolo, and Zach Meyer.

Introduction

In my first student ministry setting, we had 9 full-time student ministry staff, 2 full-time administrative staff, and 10 additional interns during the summers. Yet, even with such a large student ministry staff, we still needed an even larger number of volunteers to reach our students and accomplish our ministry plans. We would see hundreds of students at our weekly programs and take even higher numbers on 7 trips in the summers, and our staff couldn't handle leading those things on our own without the help of volunteers.

We had volunteers who faithfully came on the same mission trips every year, hosted student prayer gatherings or summer programs in their homes, led worship at youth group programs, showed up each week to meet with students in small groups, and more. Without their service, our student ministry wouldn't have had the capacity to host so many students. Without them, students would've fallen through the cracks, discipline issues would have multiplied during ministry events, and many of our staple trips and events would've been missing some vital needs.

Yet, as vital as volunteers are to ministry, we all know our share of frustrations with volunteers as well. Perhaps you can relate to one or more of these scenarios I've faced:

- You have a volunteer who almost forgets to show up to help lead a small group most weeks. If someone didn't text her each Wednesday, you're not sure she'd be there.

- You have a few volunteers who are in conflict with one another, and the students have noticed the tension.
- You have an upcoming trip, and you've asked over 40 people, yet you still can't find enough leaders. If you don't find another leader soon, you won't be able to take all the students who have registered.
- During a middle school camp, one of your volunteers breaks down in tears, because leading middle school students is tougher than she anticipated. This leader diverts your staff's attention during the trip, and afterwards this leads to reconsidering whether leading middle school students is a good fit for her (spoiler alert: it's not).
- You need more volunteers for your weekly programs, but right now the only person interested in joining is a dad who kinda gives you the creeps.
- In the middle of a youth event, you're about to go connect with students on the periphery. But suddenly, a volunteer grabs you and asks you for input on what they need to be doing. You start wondering, "Didn't they read the e-mail I sent with instructions? How hard can it be to understand how to scoop ice cream?"
- You have volunteers who are faithful to show up, but seem to consistently struggle with how to engage with students during programming. Instead, they hang at the back of the room and start conversations with you or other leaders, leading to even more of the adults being distracted from engaging with students.

In the course of student ministry, working with volunteers is both essential and difficult. They can be the source of some of the greatest encouragements and roughest challenges in your ministry. In all my time in student ministry, I never felt like I gained a level of mastery in working with volunteers, and as I have talked with other student ministers, I have noticed that many feel the same way. Because of this tension, we have endeavored to create a resource that might serve you as you seek to improve this area of your ministry.

Often when it comes to volunteers in student ministry, we can fall into a rut. We don't know what we're doing, or we don't know what else we could do. If we had new ideas and perspectives outside of our own, that might help us get unstuck. Therefore, I hope to share ideas which you can directly implement or which spark your own further thoughts.

That said, understand that this pocket guide is not meant to present a cohesive game plan for how you should go about working with volunteers in your student ministry. There are other books that do that – and they might be helpful to you. Instead, the ideas I share here are a collection which come from many sources. What works well in one context will not always work well in another. Therefore, I am not proposing that you adopt any one philosophy or strategy for your volunteers. You will need to understand your own context, decide on your own priorities, and develop your own philosophy and strategy for working with volunteers in your student ministry. Additionally, you should not implement all of the ideas in this book. Some of them will even contradict or not work well with others. Rather, it'd be better for you to see this book more as a "pick and choose what works for you" menu. Pick and test a few ideas to see what works best for your ministry, and then perhaps come back and try more if needed.

May God use this resource to help you improve your volunteer ministry and multiply your kingdom impact as a result!

1
What Are Volunteers, and Why Do You Need Them?

What is a volunteer? Merriam-Webster defines a volunteer as "a person who voluntarily undertakes or expresses a willingness to undertake a service." In other words, volunteers are those who freely choose to serve.

In ministry, volunteers are people you and God have invited to share in ministry. They're not just providing manpower or extra supervision to control chaos. They are stepping up to partner with you in reaching students and fulfilling the call to do their part as members of the body of Christ.

Perhaps when I mention volunteers, your mind goes primarily to one specific role within your student ministry. Consider, though, that volunteers can serve in many ways:

- Leading or co-leading a weekly student small group
- Assisting with setup or teardown of events
- Joining a committee of parents that helps guide the ministry
- Hosting youth events at their home
- Providing and/or serving a meal at youth events
- Participating as a leader in a student ministry trip
- Teaching a Sunday school class, whether once or often
- Helping run the AV or tech aspects of youth group
- Leading a game during youth group
- Leading worship songs during youth group

- Leading a team of students who lead the games, tech, or worship during youth group
- Driving vehicles full of students and leaders for youth group events
- Running a registration/check-in table at youth events
- Recruiting volunteers for a big youth group event
- Assisting with behind the scenes details such as sorting T-shirts, constructing folders for leaders, or cutting and organizing signs for retreats
- Praying with or for students and leaders
- Taking professional quality photos or videos during youth events
- Designing graphics for youth group events, announcements, and T-shirts
- Picking up food or supplies for youth group events
- Assisting with rethinking and redoing the design and function of the student ministry space
- Carrying out administrative tasks, such as recording attendance, typing ministry newsletters, or keeping staff on track with the upcoming needs of the ministry calendar

In ministry, it's not uncommon for staff to be doing a lot of ministry tasks and overlooking many ways that volunteers can be invited to contribute. If it's your tendency to do most of the ministry yourself, rethink this! This doesn't mean you should start delegating everything that you don't want to do to your volunteers — that could potentially drive away your volunteers, unless they happen to love the tasks that you dislike. However, we do often need to broaden our perspective when it comes to what volunteers can do and what their roles could look like.

One of the common frustrations with volunteers is that they often make our jobs more complicated. It's very easy to think, "This would get done more quickly and be done better if I just did it myself," and to therefore move forward without involving volunteers in many parts of your ministry. While in one sense things may be quicker, better, and even easier by doing things yourself, there are many reasons why we ought to reconsider this posture.

So why is it that we need volunteers? Consider these 12 reasons:

1. **You are limited in your time.** Like Moses and the apostles, you cannot do it all without wearing yourself out or dropping important priorities (Exodus 18:13-26, Acts 6:1-7).
2. **You are limited in your personality.** As much as we would like to think that we have the social skills to win over everyone, we simply don't. You will need leaders with different gifts and personalities to connect with the students that you cannot reach as well.
3. **You have weaknesses.** You cannot be strong and gifted in every area. Having others involved in leading the ministry will help offset your weaknesses as they bring their gifts to the table as well.
4. **You will not always be around.** One day, God will call you away from this ministry. Whether that's sooner or later, volunteer leaders can stick around even when you leave, providing continuity and stability to students and the ministry.
5. **You can't do ministry alone.** You need community and co-laborers around you in ministry. You and the

ministry will be better for it. Ministry isn't a solo gig, just as the Christian life isn't a solo endeavor.

6. **Student ministry is the work of the body of Christ.** God calls his covenant community to tell the coming generations about the Lord. This doesn't just mean hiring a few people to reach students. It means that families and church members from multiple generations are God's plan for equipping the next generation.
7. **Students need to see diversity in the body of Christ.** When they see volunteer leaders with different kinds of gifts who are serving in different ways, students can begin to get a picture of what it looks like for every part of the body of Christ to be doing their part to build up the body (1 Corinthians 12:12-27). This can build their understanding of how they can serve and contribute to the body as well.
8. **Students need multiple examples of Godly adulthood.** To become godly adults, students need examples to emulate. The more examples you put before them, the more they may learn about what to emulate.
9. **Involving volunteers expands your ministry.** Bringing on volunteers means that the manpower of your ministry increases, which means you can reach more students. Additionally, when you invite volunteers to contribute to the ministry, you're not only reaching the students. You're also investing more broadly in your congregation.
10. **Involving volunteers builds relationships and trust.** When you ask someone to take on a

responsibility within your ministry, you're taking a risk. In taking that risk, you're building that person's relationship with you and with the church.

11. **Ministry leadership means equipping others to do ministry.** In Ephesians 4:11-16, we see that God's design for maturity in the body is for each part to do its work. This happens as ministry leaders "equip the saints for the work of ministry, for the building up of the body of Christ" (verse 12). Therefore, ministry leadership isn't just about doing ministry yourself; it's also about equipping others to do ministry, too.
12. **Leading volunteers will give your faith room to grow.** When you entrust ministry needs to volunteers, you are giving up control. While this can be stressful, it also puts you in a place where you can learn to trust God with the results rather than trying to do everything in your own power.

2

Mistakes with Volunteers

Perhaps you've picked up this book because you know you've dropped the ball with volunteers before and you want to get better at it. You're not alone in this. I asked many student ministry workers, "What are some of the big mistakes you've made in working with volunteers?" Some of the most common themes – and the advice they would give to others – were:

1. **Recruiting volunteers carelessly**
    - Don't recruit out of desperation. This can send a bad narrative and result in accepting poor candidates.
    - Don't fall into the trap of prioritizing charisma over character, putting someone in leadership too quickly, not vetting candidates well enough, or taking anyone who is willing to volunteer. Some people may initially look like they'd be great volunteers, but their poorly developed character will lead to bad outcomes. Make sure they're ready for leadership.
    - Take time to discern fit before offering someone a role. In some cases, the student ministry may simply not be the best fit for someone's gifts, and there may be a better place in the church for them to serve.
    - Be careful about who you put in volunteer roles. If you don't do a good job vetting them, you will

eventually have to do the much harder task of taking leadership away from them.

2. **Not giving volunteers clarity around roles and expectations**
    - A lack of clarity leads to misunderstandings and issues.
    - Have clear, concise, written job descriptions for your volunteers. Create sample job descriptions even for potential roles that are not currently filled, so that these will be available if/when you need them.
    - Don't assume clarity without checking for it. Don't expect volunteers to read your mind.
    - Keep the vision, values, and expectations before your volunteers. You can't over-communicate these things.
3. **Poor communication with volunteers**
    - Many student ministry leaders regret not communicating more regularly with their volunteers, whether that meant something as simple as regular email updates or one-on-one conversations with volunteers.
    - Other mistakes included waiting too long to communicate with volunteers or not listening well to volunteers.
    - Failing to check in regularly with volunteers can also lead to a lot of issues and regrets. Don't assume that they don't need check-ins from you. It's better to check in and hear that everything is good than to assume as much and be wrong.
4. **Failing to address issues with volunteers**

- Don't avoid hard conversations with volunteers. The longer you wait, the more damage can be done as small problems turn into bigger ones. Keeping a bad leader around can let them continue to create a bad culture in the student ministry.

5. **Neglecting the importance of volunteers**
    - It's easy to get caught up in reaching students yourself and forget that student ministry is not just about how well you can reach the students. It's also about raising up a team of volunteers from the church to reach the students.
    - Beware of not taking it seriously that it's your job to recruit, equip, coach, and encourage your volunteers. This is a regular, multiple-hours per week, essential part of your job, not just something to focus on occasionally when you find yourself needing more volunteers or particular issues arise.
    - Volunteers are people God has entrusted to your care, just as much as the students you are ministering to. Invest in them, and the ministry will become richer and healthier.

3

Recruiting Volunteers

Rather than falling into common mistakes with volunteers, I want to help you adopt some best practices. Throughout the rest of this resource, I will be sharing ideas for best practices throughout the major parts of your work with volunteers. The first of these parts is recruiting volunteers.

Recruiting volunteers is a large pain point for many student ministries. It's also something that a lot of ministry leaders lack skill and training for. **If there's one place to start in improving your recruiting approach, it may be to give more of your time to recruitment and have a plan for it**. If you need to find more volunteers, plan to put time aside for recruiting regularly. The more time you set aside, the more quickly you will see success. However much time you already devote to recruiting volunteers, increase it. Try to start with at least 2 hours per week.

Once you have that time set aside, you need to know what to do with it. Let's break down recruitment into several pieces.

Identifying Needs

First, **start with identifying the needs within your ministry**. Do you need small group leaders? A worship leader? People to help with check-in or crowd control? You can use the previous list of ways volunteers can be serving as a starting point if you need ideas. Knowing what volunteers you need helps you identify the right people. **Consider breaking down your needs into a few categories**:

- high-touch discipling volunteers (such small group leaders or any volunteer who does relational ministry)
- specially skilled volunteers (worship leader, photographer, graphic designer, etc.)
- events volunteers (those who can help with crowd control, flipping pancakes, running registration, etc.)
- behind-the-scenes volunteers (parent committee, administrative helpers, etc.).

Another way to think through your needs is to shift from identifying tasks or roles that need filling to **identifying needs from the perspective of your philosophy of ministry**. Perhaps you believe in the importance of covenant community, intergenerational connection, and integration into the greater church body, but your student ministry has considerable gaps in these areas, and recruiting the right volunteers would help fill those gaps. Maybe your current volunteers all lean toward one perspective or set of gifts, and you want to add other voices and provide your students with a more diverse set of Godly examples. Consider how your philosophy of ministry informs who you are looking for as volunteers.

Also identify how many volunteers you are in need of. This may seem obvious, but putting that number down on paper can help you establish a clear goal to work toward and keep your eye on the ball as you go through the difficult process of recruiting volunteers.

Some of the most important volunteers are the high-touch discipling volunteers, who will be significantly involved in the student ministry and in the lives of students. They may primarily fill just one role, such as a small group leader, or they may do many different things for the ministry. Throughout the rest of this guide, most of the ideas shared will apply most directly to working with these kinds of volunteers. However, don't forget about the other volunteers, too. They may only show up from time to time to serve in your ministry in smaller ways, such as providing a meal or being an extra set of hands for a larger event, but their smaller contributions help your ministry run smoothly and increase your impact as well.

Who To Recruit

It's hard to find enough leaders, and sometimes that leads us to want to accept anyone who is breathing and willing to volunteer. Because volunteers have a huge influence on our ministries, though, we need to be careful. How should we think through who to recruit, then? Some of the best practices include:

1. **Define what you're looking for**. What kind of person do you want? When I asked student ministry leaders what they look for in volunteers, they pointed to the following qualities which you can consider:
    - Character & Spiritual Maturity
        - Godliness and love for the Lord
        - The kind of people that you would like your teens to emulate
        - Joy and confidence in Christ
        - Committed to the church
        - Teachable and humble
        - Gracious
        - Practicing their own soul care
        - Being discipled by someone more mature than them

        - Knows their testimony
        - Can communicate the Gospel
    - Relational & Social Skills
        - Love for people, relational skills, warmth, and presence
        - Able to enter into youth culture and relate well to students
        - Fun/funny/willing to be goofy
        - Discerning in how they relate to students and parents
        - Socially and emotionally aware and healthy (and won't look to students for their own needs)
    - Reliability and Commitment
        - Dependable and committed
        - Potentially committed for long-haul ministry, not just short-term enthusiasm
        - Has the margin/capacity to make this commitment; isn't already serving in a lot of other ways
    - Team Dynamics
        - Passionate
        - Flexible
        - Personality that complements/differs from others on current volunteer team (in order to build a team that reaches a variety of student personalities)
2. **Look for strengths and attitudes over skills.** For most roles, your candidates don't have to already be skilled. You can teach them the skills to lead small groups or teach lessons, for example. Instead, focus on

the qualities you want them to have which aren't as easy to teach.

3. **Keep in mind any requirements you may have for volunteer candidates.** For example, many churches follow the practice of requiring volunteers to have been a communing member of the church for at least 6 months prior to volunteering in the youth group. This will narrow down your pool of potential candidates.
4. **Reconsider your assumptions about who might be good for the roles you need.** Maybe you naturally picture someone of a certain age, personality, or stage of life when recruiting for certain volunteer roles. Take some time to broaden your perspective and consider people outside of that category. Someone who is more introverted, for example, may be great at connecting with your introverted students.

On that last point, here are a few stage of life categories and some pros and cons that might come with having them as student ministry volunteers:

- Parents of Students
    - Pros: They already are familiar with teens, since they are raising at least one. Having parents volunteering will also build your partnership with them.
    - Cons: Their kids might want or need space from them. Some students might not be sure about opening up to another parent.
- Empty Nesters

    - Pros: They are likely to have more freedom in their schedules, as well as wisdom from having raised teens.
    - Cons: They may feel they are "too old" or need help relating to teens.
- College Students
    - Pros: They are usually full of energy and likely to naturally relate well to middle and high school students, having recently been one themselves.
    - Cons: They have less maturity than older adults, and this may lead to more issues you need to address with them.
- Young Parents
    - Pros: They may be in a "sweet spot" in terms of still being young enough to easily relate well and seem "cool" to students while also being old enough to have gained more maturity in their faith.
    - Cons: When their kids are young, life may be crazy for them, and they may not have as much availability and flexibility.
- High School Students
    - Pros: Letting them serve as leaders to middle school students can be a great opportunity for further discipleship and leadership. They will often connect very naturally with middle school students.
    - Cons: If their younger sibling is in middle school, that may put limits around the best spaces for them to serve. They will also be immature, and you may have to address more issues with them.

Finding Leads

Recruiting volunteers is something you can — and maybe should — be doing year round. Don't wait until it's time to start a new ministry calendar year to think about recruiting new volunteers. You might even want to develop a formal or informal recruitment pipeline. You can be laying seeds or bringing people through different stages in your recruiting process throughout the whole year.

How do you find the people to do this with, though? You need to **create a list of potential leads**. For everyone who comes to mind that might be a good volunteer candidate, write their name down. Here are some ways to approach this when no one comes to the top of your mind:

1. **Start with internal sourcing.**
    - Brainstorm a list of people from your church to ask. Have you noticed any adults in your congregation that fit the description of what you are looking for in a volunteer? Or anyone who already seems to be organically connecting with teenagers?
    - Sit down with your church directory and identify more people who might make a good volunteer.
    - Look amongst newer members of your church who haven't yet found a place to serve.
2. **Use networking approaches.**
    - When you need more leads beyond the people you know, approach it like networking. Let others in your church know you have a need for more volunteers. Ask others for their help identifying

leads. Ask your students, current volunteers, other ministry leaders and church officers, parents of teens, leaders of adult classes and small groups, and so on. Let them know you are looking for people in the church who are Godly and who are the kind of people they would want influencing the teens.

    - Side note: you can also encourage these people to encourage those they think would be good candidates. It could mean a lot for a potential volunteer to hear a student tell them they would be a great small group leader, for instance, and this would lay some seeds for you in the recruiting process.

  - Your current volunteers might have good answers to the question, "Who else do you think might be good at doing what you've been doing in the student ministry?"
  - Even when it gets tough (and you've asked 40 different people), don't give up. I've faced the situation where I thought I had exhausted all my connections and leads many times. But when I would go back to the drawing board, I would come up with more people to ask to help me find leads. God always came through.

3. **Use and develop organic recruiting methods.**
  - Sometimes it can be as simple as inviting your friends or encouraging your volunteers to invite their friends to consider serving in the student ministry. As a bonus, this can help build a team with strong relationships.

- When you need more high-touch discipling volunteers like small group leaders, remember to also look amongst your current list of other types of volunteers. Often someone who has been already serving in smaller ways in your student ministry could very naturally take the next step and become more engaged with students in a larger role.
- Some of the best recruiting can happen organically, as news spreads that volunteering with the student ministry is enjoyable. Find ways to highlight to others the impact that your volunteers are having and how fun student ministry is, such as sharing pictures of volunteers with students. Encourage your current volunteers to invite others to volunteer as well and tell them about what the experience has been like. At some point, people will start knocking on your door rather than the other way around.

4. **Pray and ask God to connect you with the right people.**
5. **Come up with as many names as you can.** You will need your list of potential volunteers to be longer than the list of volunteer roles you need filled, because many people will say "no." If you don't make it all the way through your list before filling your current needs, you can save the list for next time.

Asking Leads

Once you have leads, the next thing you need to do is ask them to consider volunteering in the student ministry. Here are some ways to approach this:

1. **Prioritize your list of leads.** Consider ranking them into a few categories (like "I'd kill to have this person as a volunteer!," "This person has good potential," or "They'd be alright.") so you can decide who you might reach out to first.
2. **Ask potential volunteers to serve well in advance of when you will need them.**
    - Recognize that many adults make other commitments to serve (on the school PTA, in professional organizations, and so on) far in advance, so you may need to ask far in advance, too.
    - You could ask people about their interest in serving even when you aren't immediately in need of volunteers. If anyone affirms interest, put their name on a list to come back to later when a need does arise.
    - For some volunteer roles, you also might consider asking someone far enough in advance to let them shadow a current leader as they discern whether or not they might take on the same role. They might sit in on a small group, attend an event, or join another leader at a student's extracurricular activity, for example.

3. **Ask people individually and personally.** This is a much more effective strategy for recruiting volunteers than a wide ask such as an announcement in a newsletter or from the pulpit. That's part of why you want to collect individual names as leads rather than just making broad announcements that you need more volunteers. These broad announcements can be appropriate at times, especially for events where you need a large number of volunteers from across the church, but when you need high-quality, highly-committed volunteers, individual asks will be a better strategy.
4. **Don't surprise people.** Don't just walk up to individuals after church service and ask them on the spot to become a small group leader or join you for a mission trip. Ask them initially to schedule a time to have a conversation with you about serving in the student ministry. All they're saying "yes" to at this point is to meet and hear about the ministry opportunity. That gives you the chance for a proper pitch.
5. **Another potential strategy is to have an "open house" or recruiting event** in which you share about the student ministry, its vision, and what it's like to be a volunteer. You can ask your current volunteers to come to this event and to invite a few people that they think would be good volunteers. Sweeten the deal by including something like free food that will entice people to come. During this event you could use your current volunteers to help paint a picture of what volunteering is like and why it's worth it, and you can

share your pitch to multiple people at once and follow up with them individually afterwards.

When it comes to your "pitch," plan ahead of time what you want to communicate. Here are some things you could consider:

1. **Sell them on a vision.** Don't just talk about what they will be doing. Tell them the *why* behind becoming a volunteer. Help them see the vision and mission of the ministry and how they can impact teens and serve God through this opportunity.
2. **Let them know why you think they might be good for the role.** If you're asking someone because you or someone else thinks they will be good for this role, tell them that. If their name was mentioned by multiple people, tell them that. Affirm what you or others see in them.
3. **Use the language of invitation.** That might sound something like, "As I was thinking about our student ministry's needs, your name came to mind (or was suggested by _____) because ______. So I want to invite you to consider joining our mission to reach students by serving as ________."
4. **Be clear about the role and expectations you are inviting them into.** Be specific about things like dates and times, hours per week, length of commitment, and any work or expectations outside of programmed times. Give them a document that outlines these expectations in writing.

    - Several student ministry leaders told me that they have shifted to asking upfront about a volunteer's willingness to stick around for several years, and that has been very beneficial to the ministry. If this is what you want, clearly ask for it!
5. **Make sure they know ways that you can provide support throughout their service.** If you provide training, the curriculum they will use with students, or additional leaders that they will co-lead with, this would be good for them to know. It will make the ask seem more manageable.
6. **If they seem interested, let them know about your process for screening and onboarding volunteers, so they know what to expect.**
7. **Let them have the opportunity to ask questions.**
8. **Encourage them to pray about the opportunity.** Emphasize that this is about whether God is calling them to serve with the student ministry.
9. **Give them time to pray, process, and get back to you before expecting an answer.** You might want to set a deadline for this and let them know you'll get in touch with them when that deadline hits.
10. **Be sure to follow up afterwards.** It is your job to make sure this happens, not the other person's.

The Screening Process

You need an organized process for screening and onboarding volunteers. However, this can be tailored to the role. If someone is merely helping run a check-in table one time at an event with many others around, the amount of screening and onboarding you need to do for them will be different than a volunteer who is highly engaged with students on a weekly basis, regularly seeks out students for relational ministry, and/or is participating in overnight events with students. These differences might be outlined in a safety policy for your church (more about this later).

Here's what a robust process might look like for the volunteers for whom you need the most screening:

1. **Start with a written (hand or digital) application.** This creates a paper trail for you, and allows you to collect important information and ask basic questions about their gifting, background, interest in serving, and more.
2. **Conduct an interview.** Focus on questions that will help you discern whether they are the right fit for volunteering in student ministry.
3. **Run a background check on applicants.** Your church should hopefully already have a system setup for this.
    - You might also at this point want to require some of your volunteers to complete a sexual abuse awareness training and turn in a certificate showing they have passed the training.
4. **Take this process seriously and prayerfully.** Just because someone goes through these steps doesn't mean they will be a good fit for serving in your student ministry. Say "no" when you need to, and redirect them to other roles that they might be better suited for. Your honest and gracious feedback can help them discover a better place for them to thrive in using their gifts.

5. **Multiple male youth directors/pastors have also recommended the practice of running volunteer applicant names by a female staff member.** They see the wisdom in relying on a woman's sense of intuition, for she may notice things about potential volunteers that he might miss.
6. **Go over expectations clearly.** At some point in this process (whether as part of the application or once they are officially "onboarding"), share with them in writing your expectations for their role and gain in writing their commitment to that before they are cleared to serve.

Obstacles

You may face a lot of challenges as you seek to find more volunteers.

Often when it's hard for the student ministry to find volunteers, it's not the only ministry in the church dealing with this issue. **One particularly difficult obstacle is when the church overall doesn't have a strong volunteering culture**. When this isn't just a student ministry issue but is a whole church issue, it can feel like climbing a mountain. Here are a few ideas to help if you're in this situation:

1. **Start small and build momentum.** You might begin by giving people short-term, lower-commitment opportunities that allow them to experience wins before asking them to take on larger commitments.
2. **Make a point of celebrating the volunteers you do have.** Publicly recognize them in whatever ways you

can. In broader church settings, talk about what's going on in the student ministry, share pictures, and highlight the impact the volunteers are having. This helps normalize the behavior that you want to see more of.

3. **Highlight "non-typical" volunteers.** This can help break down people's misunderstandings of what it takes to be a good student ministry volunteer.
4. **Talk with pastors and ministry leaders in your church about how you can work together to encourage more volunteerism in your church.** This may include teaching the whole church in order to shift their perspective (about their responsibilities as covenant family members to help disciple the next generation, for example) or creating pathways to funnel new members into volunteering opportunities.
5. **Design and implement a good plan for recruiting and leading volunteers.** The apparent lack of a volunteering culture at your church could simply be because no one on staff is skilled in the area of recruiting and leading volunteers.
6. **If possible, look at the stats on volunteering in your church as a whole to identify possible weak spots.** For example, Nick Blevins, in his book *The Volunteer Playbook,* writes about how he took inventory in his church and discovered that there were over 75 existing teams of volunteers – far too many for a church with only 300 adults![1]

---

1. Nick Blevins, *The Volunteer Playbook* (Nick Blevins, 2023), 173-5.

Another issue you will face is people declining the invitation to volunteer. How you handle their "no" can help set you up for future success. For instance, you could:

1. **Say, "That's okay. Thanks for considering. Expect to hear from me again next year."** It could be that next year will be better timing for them, or that God will move their heart between now and then. If there's someone you really want to add to your team, you can keep asking them over time!
2. **Ask them to consider other opportunities.** Maybe they can't make a weekly commitment to lead a small group right now, but they'd be interested in helping out occasionally with special events, teaching a Sunday school lesson a couple times a year, or serving on a committee. Let them dip their toes in the water until they're able to commit to more, and in this way they may later be able to make a larger commitment at a time when they already have some familiarity with the students.
3. **Ask them if there's another way or time they'd like to serve.** Maybe they have an idea for a different role they could fulfill, or maybe they know that in 6 months they might be more available.

4
Training Volunteers

You want your volunteers to be equipped, and your volunteers will want to feel equipped for the roles you give them. Many of your volunteers may come with little to no experience leading in ministries or working directly with teens. Therefore, **training your volunteers is an essential part of helping set up them and the student ministry for success.**

In fact, all that you do in training and coaching your volunteers can be part of a "secret sauce" for your ministry thriving. Does it seem like most of your volunteers are weak in one area? You can help them grow through training targeted at that weakness. Are you finding it hard to recruit volunteers with the skills you're hoping for? Remember that you can help recruits develop those skills through training and mentoring. **You have the ability to shape and form the kinds of volunteers you want for the student ministry** – because training is not just about giving them the right information, but about forming leaders who can effectively and sustainably reach teens with the Gospel.

Don't be surprised if not all of your volunteers attend. **You may need to teach them the importance of attending training sessions.** A few things you can do to increase participation include feeding them, providing childcare, picking a time that works well for your volunteers, and having a good RSVP process. Make sure your leaders know far in advance when your trainings are, and ask them to RSVP. If they don't show or don't RSVP, graciously hold them accountable. If you don't, you may be sending the message that their attendance doesn't really matter.

The Right Amount of Training

When you plan for training your volunteers, **think carefully about your load of training**. You need to train your volunteers well, and also beware of overloading them with training. A new volunteer may immediately regret their decision if they join your team and find out that they are going to be overwhelmed with content and meetings. Remember that this is not their job, and that they have many responsibilities outside of their time volunteering for the student ministry. Here are some ways to think through training load:

- **Aim for that "just right" spot between too much and too little training** in terms of the frequency and length of your trainings and the content you pass on to them.
- **Every ministry will find that a different frequency of training works best for them.** Meeting for training anywhere from one to four times a semester seems to be pretty normal. Finding the frequency that works for your ministry may take some trial and error. Some models that work for different student ministries include:
    - A once a month leaders' meal (in some ministries, this replaces youth group that week)
    - One or two mandatory training sessions per semester with essential information, and additional trainings that are encouraged but not required
    - You could also ask your current volunteers for their input on frequency – build out a potential meeting schedule for the coming semester or year,

then float that plan to them and ask for their feedback

- **The timing and format of your training also matters, too.**
  - A common format is a 1-2 hour meeting with volunteers for training.
  - You could also utilize huddles (10-15 minute meetings) before or after youth group every week, which provides more frequent but shorter training sessions.
  - You might consider scheduling your training sessions to be right after another event that your volunteers would likely already be at (like after your Sunday worship service) or at the same time you would normally have youth group.
  - You can offer some of your training online or on-demand. Consider using Zoom meetings in the evenings, or recording short videos that you ask them to watch in their own time with a deadline attached.

In addition to training meetings, you can encourage leaders to grow on their own time and pursue more training as they can. Some leaders may enthusiastically pursue these opportunities, while others won't have the time, and that is okay. Toward this end, some ideas you could use include:

1. **Pass on podcast episodes and online articles relevant to student ministry to your volunteers via email or text.** Consider resources from ministries like RYM, CPYU, and Axis.

2. **Recommend books to your volunteers.** Even better, if your ministry budget allows it, suggest a book and tell them to let you know if they want a copy so you can buy it for them. It's a small way to invest in their growth.
3. **Gift your volunteers a book without requiring them to read it.** Let them get to it in their own time.[1]
4. **If you attend a conference or training event for student ministry leaders, invite one or more of your most committed volunteers to come along with you.** Just make sure you budget for this!

The Content of Training

It's one thing to plan times for training, and another thing to decide what you will train your volunteers in. These points may guide your decisions in the content of training:

1. **Consider designing an onboarding experience and/or training module specifically for new volunteers.** Maybe there's a special orientation training session at the beginning of their service and/or a series of conversations and check-ins for coaching and encouragement with you, before joining the normal rotation of training with all the other volunteers.
2. **If your recruiting and screening process didn't already cover it, you need to establish clear expectations for your volunteers in their initial**

1. Try Mike McGarry's *Lead Them to Jesus: A Handbook for Youth Workers,* which was originally written for his own student ministry volunteers.

training. Most commonly, this is done through a written job description for their role – either one that you create yourself or one that you co-create with the volunteer. This clarity will help both them and the ministry in so many ways, and can help prevent further issues down the road.

3. **At a minimum, you need to train your leaders to do what you are asking them to do.** For example, if they are leading a small group, walk them through what their small group time will look like and how to lead that time, including how to use the curriculum and pointers for leading prayer time.
4. **Volunteers also need to know your policies.** Go through any policy documents that pertain to working with minors within your church setting. Because these can be long and tedious, you might consider giving them a copy to read through on their own time and then hitting the highlights with them. You could also cover this in-depth once in a volunteer's onboarding process, and then revisit it with all of your leaders once a year through briefer discussions or case studies.
5. **Often people need to hear something multiple times, so don't be afraid to repeat yourself** in order to provide clarity about what they are called to do, how they are going to do it, and why they are serving. Keep the vision and the expectations before them.
6. **Make sure that you make training worth your volunteers' time.** Training should have a clear focus and be engaging.
7. Outside of the minimum and required training needs, there's plenty more you can train your volunteers in.

What you decide to cover should depend on your needs, context, and leaders. Consider the different skill levels and weaknesses of your leaders. Make sure the topic will land as practical and relevant with them.

8. **Some topics you might consider for training include:**
    - Ministry philosophy
    - Your student ministry's vision, values, and strategy
    - Relational ministry and connecting with students
    - Listening skills
    - Being Jesus-centered/gospel-centered in teaching and conversations
    - Biblical theology/the narrative of Scripture
    - Partnering with parents
    - Understanding generational differences
    - Understanding current teen culture topics and trends
    - Mental health
    - Adolescent development
    - Handling discipline with students
    - Handling conflict between students
    - Responding to tough questions from students
    - Procedures for tough situations with students (crises, abuse, mandatory reporting, etc.)
    - Healthy boundaries
9. **Let your philosophy of ministry inform how you train your volunteers.** For your student ministry to have deep, theological roots, make sure your training includes topics around this and doesn't only focus around strategies and methodologies.

10. **Consider pursuing more training yourself, so that you can pass the things you are learning onto your volunteers.**
11. When you get together with your volunteer leaders, design that time well. **In addition to training content, maybe you want to include time for**:
    - Serving them free food or coffee (If you have the ability, make it good! Don't just throw the cheapest pizza at your volunteers every time.)
    - Building relationships with and amongst your volunteers
    - Discussion of concerns
    - Celebration of ministry wins
    - Evaluation of how their role is going
    - Collection of feedback from your volunteers
    - Praying for the ministry and students
12. **A few effective tips or strategies worth trying in training include:**
    - **Use the model of Tell, Show, Do, Lead.** First, tell them what to do. Next, show them what to do -- let them watch you do what you just told them to do. Afterwards, do the thing together with them. Finally, release them to lead that thing on their own, perhaps first with a trial of you watching them to assist and offer feedback as needed. This can take place over a short or long period of time for various skills.
    - **Give them extra encouragement to break the ice with students.** Ask your volunteers about how they perceived themselves in middle or high school, what kind of group they would have fit in

with, and/or to use one word to describe themselves at that age. This can help them identify students that they may be able to relate to most easily, as well as the ones they might avoid, whether intentionally or unintentionally. Encourage them to be aware of this, and to make an effort to speak to those they might tend to avoid, even if it's brief.

- **Consider having your volunteers set specific and attainable goals,** such as: "I will learn the names of everyone in my small group in the next 2 weeks," or "I will invite one student from my small group to get ice cream next week." These can be especially helpful in the area of training and encouraging volunteers to build relationships with students. You can use training time or one-on-ones with your volunteers to check in on these goals.

5
Leading Volunteers

Outside of training your volunteers, there is also **the important and ongoing work of leading your volunteers.** This will be less formal than planned training times, and it can often be used to help the leaders genuinely grow in the things you have trained them in. In many ways, then, it is an extension of training. At the same time, leading your volunteers well goes beyond developing their skills. It's also about managing them as people and providing the guidance and direction they need.

As you lead your volunteers, they will need a challenge (a task you've given them to do), support (the resources needed to complete the task), and encouragement (affirmation and coaching along the way). A clear task can be defined in their volunteer job description; support is often provided through training; and encouragement comes through your leadership and management, which we will discuss in this section. By default, most of us tend to leave a gap in one of these three areas – so notice your weakness and be intentional to close the gap!

An essential piece to leading your volunteers is building relationships with them. Without relationships, it will be more difficult to lead your volunteers well and get the best out of them. Usually the volunteers who are most relationally engaged with you will also be most invested in the ministry. So, make it your first priority to build strong relationships with your volunteers as people. Get to know them and gain their trust through showing you care. Be willing to be vulnerable about your own ministry struggles, and point them to Jesus rather than to yourself.

Coaching and Mentoring

Your volunteers will need ongoing coaching and mentoring from you. Here are some pointers for this area:

1. **Pay attention to specific coaching and mentoring needs when a volunteer is new or taking on new responsibilities.**
   a. When a new volunteer comes on board, meet with them after a specific time – maybe 6 weeks or so, depending on the role – to check in, get feedback, and help them in any needed areas.
   b. You could have a new volunteer apprentice under a more experienced volunteer for a semester or two.
   c. You can provide "on the job" training for newer volunteers. Invite them to come along with you to relational ministry and extracurriculars for students or to study a passage with you as you prepare and shape an upcoming lesson, for instance.
2. **Meet with your volunteers regularly to check in, coach, encourage, and mentor them.** Consider setting pre-defined check-in dates, which create a natural opportunity for evaluation and give both you and them a guilt-free off-ramp when it's time to shift roles or step away. Maybe once a year you could have them do a short self-evaluation that will help you know how to best support them in the coming year.
3. **Expect that your volunteers will need follow up and coaching even after you train them in specific topics.** They are learning as they go. It's your job to

regularly encourage them in order to reinforce what they're doing well and to provide constructive feedback as needed in order for them to course-correct and improve.

4. **Notice your volunteer's gifts and strengths, and speak into these regularly.** This is a deeply valuable relational skill as you lead your volunteers, so put effort into developing and using this skill.
5. **As you provide feedback and coaching, adopt a posture that is constructive, helpful, and growth-oriented.** Make sure the volunteer knows you genuinely want to see them succeed and grow into their potential, and that you are not trying to make them feel like a failure when you point out something that needs improvement. If this kind of mindset and giving feedback in this way is challenging for you, consider working with a coach or mentor who can help you grow in this.
6. **Notice whether your volunteers make a habit of regularly communicating with you or feel comfortable bringing needs and questions to you.** If this isn't the case, ask for feedback from your volunteers or others about the reasons why. Endeavor to make yourself approachable and available to them.
7. **Provide your volunteers with spiritual care and disciple them.** This will make them feel valued as persons. Soul care is essential for your leaders, and investing in their spiritual health is ultimately an investment in the spiritual health of your students as well, since your volunteers' spiritual health will determine what they pass on to students.

8. **Depending on the size of your volunteer team, you may need more than one person involved in this process.** The more volunteers you have, the more doing this well will become beyond your capacity. If you have other student ministry staff members, have them share the load. If you don't, consider training one or more of your volunteers to be a leader amongst the volunteers and help do some of the work of coaching and mentoring others.

Building Culture and Community

Pay attention to the culture and community that exists amongst your volunteers. The way you train and spend time with your volunteers will build relationships and a set of cultural norms within your ministry and volunteer base. Some ideas you could utilize include:

1. **Regularly share stories in your volunteer team of how God is at work**. This helps them keep God's work at the forefront and builds a culture of celebration.
2. **Use team building activities with your volunteers** to facilitate stronger relationships and teamwork.
3. **At least once a year, plan something with your volunteers that allows a lot more time than usual for relationship building.** This could range from a casual dinner or a fun outing to an overnight retreat with your volunteers.
4. **Assess the level of community amongst your volunteers.** What are their relationships with each

other like? Identify where there are needs and take steps to facilitate community. Building community amongst them is a great retention strategy, too.

5. **Key in on the values you want to define the culture amongst your volunteers.** Make a list of these values and share them with your volunteers. Gently correct them when they go against these values. For any of these values that your team is currently weak in, come up with action steps you can take to build on them over time.
6. **Assess the culture amongst your volunteers.** What are the assumptions and norms of the group? How would you put words to the values that your team currently demonstrates? Notice places where the weaknesses amongst your volunteer team may not be due to a lack of skills but due to a culture that you need to shift the needle on over time.
7. Many student ministries have enjoyed and benefitted from **having regular or spontaneous outings with their volunteers immediately after youth events**. Grabbing a meal or drinks with volunteers after youth group can be a great way to build relationships and informally celebrate and debrief.
8. **Find ways to make a great team environment that others will want to be a part of.** If your current volunteers feel that being part of the student ministry team is a blast and feel a sense of purpose in their service, this kind of culture may do a lot of the recruitment work for you. In other words, word may spread, and others may be coming to you to ask to be a

part of the team, and this culture will likely continue to self-replicate.

9. Culture is something that is seen and experienced. **You need to model to your volunteers the culture you want them to adopt.**

Questions Worth Asking Your Volunteers

When you meet with volunteers in groups or one on one, be intentional in the conversations you have with them. In addition to majoring in encouragement and affirming what they are doing well, **ask good questions**. Come to that conversation with questions in mind, or send them questions ahead of time to think on. When I asked student ministry leaders for some of the best questions they ask their volunteers, they shared the following:

- **About ministry to students:**
    - What needs are you seeing amongst the students?
    - What did you learn about a student this week?
    - What students are you connecting best with?
    - What significant conversations have you had with students or their parents in the past (time frame)?
    - What kinds of questions are students asking you?
    - What Scripture are you using in (name a situation) with (student)?
    - What are some barriers you're facing in getting together with students for relational ministry?
- **About their ministry leadership:**
    - What are some wins you've seen over the last (time frame)? Losses?
    - What are you enjoying about ministry?

  - Where do you feel most confident in your role? Where do you feel unsure, frustrated, or stuck?
  - What are ways that you feel stressed because you're tempted to think you need to be God for your students?
  - What's the hardest part of your role? What's the most fulfilling?
  - What are some areas where you want to improve?
  - What training would you like to have? Do you feel equipped by the content and training you are provided with? Are there any topics you would like resources on?
  - What do you need from me? How can I help you succeed? How can I better support you? How can I encourage you?
  - How can I pray for you in your ministry?
  - Is there anything we're doing as a team that's making it harder for you to lead well?
  - What is the dynamic with your co-leader like?
  - What would seem like too much for me to ask of you, and what would seem like too little?
  - How can I improve communication with you as a volunteer?
  - Do you believe your gifts were utilized this past (time frame)?
  - What would make you excited to volunteer again? Hesitant to volunteer again?
- **About the student ministry overall:**
  - If you could change one thing about how we do youth group, what would it be?

    - What are some ways you're seeing God moving in the ministry?
    - What am I (as the leader) missing? Is there something that would be helpful for me to know?
    - What are we doing well?
    - What can we do better?
    - What would you do differently?
- **About their personal life:**
    - What's going on in your life – family, friends, work, etc.?
    - How is your regular time with God going?
    - What are some ways you're seeing God moving in your personal life?
    - How can I be praying for you in your personal life?
    - What's been life-giving for you lately?
    - What aspects of your calling as a parent/spouse/in your career feel like they are bumping up against your calling to do student ministry?
    - When was the last time you took a day and rested?
    - Who is pouring into you as you pour into students?
    - What determines your identity?

Communicating Consistently

Managing volunteers well means you must be communicating well with them. Here are some points to help you think about good communication:

1. **Make sure you are clear with your volunteers about what's going on in the ministry and what**

you're expecting of them. Without clear and consistent communication, volunteers are left in the dark about what's going on in the ministry and how they can best serve.

2. **Ensure your volunteers have the necessary information for their roles.** In some cases, weekly communication will be necessary. This may be regular emails with a few pointers about the upcoming small group lesson or a brief leader huddle before youth group to get on the same page about details.
3. **If communication is something you easily overlook, set yourself recurring reminders to do this for your volunteers.** They need this consistency from you.
4. Communication is a two-way street. **Volunteers also need to know how they can communicate with you.** Let them know how they can bring up issues, questions, or feedback. Don't wait til the end of the semester to hear their thoughts about how things are going when you could have the opportunity to address and help volunteers resolve issues sooner than that.
5. **Let your communication consistently involve encouragement as well.** Regularly affirming your volunteers will go a long way in developing your relationship with them, building a culture of noticing one another's gifts, and promoting longevity. It will also give you a good foundation upon which you can address issues or weaknesses when needed.

Encouraging Relational Ministry

Ministry is most effective in the context of strong relationships. Therefore, **having volunteers engage in relational ministry with students can massively increase their impact.** However, asking and getting volunteers to get together with students outside of programs is very different than getting them to show up to lead a small group. **If you're looking to encourage your volunteer team to do more relational ministry, borrow from these ideas:**

1. **If you can get one volunteer who is great at this, it may inspire others.**
2. **Set a vision and expectation about relational ministry.**
    - Give your volunteers a vision for relational ministry. Share stories that show the kind of relationships and impact they can have with students through relational ministry over the long haul. Cast a vision for how it can impact their own life as a leader, too.
    - Help your volunteers have realistic expectations about relational ministry. Let them know that building a relationship will take months and can feel awkward at first.
    - When recruiting volunteers, talk with them upfront about relational ministry. Ask how much they might be able to do this before they commit.
3. **Train them well for relational ministry.**
    - Expect leaders to need training and mentoring in relational ministry, and offer it.

    - Give your leaders suggestions for what to do for contact work.
    - Encourage them to start small. Even a quick text asking for prayer requests, a 5-minute phone call, or a short letter to a student can go a long way in building a relationship.
    - For busy adult volunteers, it may be helpful to suggest ways they can "stack" their responsibilities, such as taking students along while completing an errand.
4. **Facilitate relationships and relational ministry for your volunteers.**
    - Help your leaders see the importance of building relationships with students' families for the purposes of relational ministry, and train them in how to do that.
    - Facilitate relationships between parents and volunteers. Try planning events or workshops that both parents and volunteers are invited to.
    - Encourage families to host their own student's small group for a casual gathering and to invite their leader(s) to join.
    - Invite your leaders to come along with you when doing relational ministry.
5. **Demonstrate relational ministry with/to your volunteers.** Send your volunteers texts to check in on them, follow up on their prayer requests, or ask them to get together for a casual outing. They can learn to do this with students as they "catch" this behavior from you doing it with them.

6. **Check in with your volunteers regularly to ask how they're doing in relational ministry and how you can help.**
7. It may feel like a lot to ask your volunteers to do relational ministry, but **you don't have to be afraid of asking them for higher commitment.** It's valuable and worth asking people to do.
8. **Give volunteers ownership in how they do relational ministry.** Encourage them to lean into their personality and interests.

6

Stewarding Volunteers

As you lead your volunteers, be intentional about being a good steward of them. **Be thoughtful and responsible as you manage them and their time and talents.** Building relationships with your volunteers is essential to stewarding them well. Additionally, pay attention to how you use them and how you encourage longevity.

How You Use Volunteers

As noted in the first section, you can use volunteers in many different roles and ways. How you use them, though, can go beyond the roles listed earlier. To broaden your thinking, consider these ideas:

1. **You can solely recruit volunteers to predefined roles. However, an alternative option is to take time with a volunteer to discern their gifts and tailor a role to them as much as possible.**
    - One way to do this is a hybrid job description. Include minimum requirements in the job description, and then have a conversation with the volunteer to give them a broad perspective on the ministry and work together to figure out what their particular contribution will be. Let the volunteer write down for themselves the rest of

their volunteer job description. This increases buy-in and can make accountability much easier.

2. **Ask yourself, are there any current volunteers who would be glad to do more if you asked them to?** What else would they be interested in doing?
3. **Use an assessment such as the StrengthsFinder, Working Genius, Predictive Index, or a spiritual gifts inventory to help discover your volunteers' strengths and better understand how to work together as a team.**
4. **In whatever role a volunteer serves, define some boundaries for them, and then encourage them to have freedom within those boundaries.** This enables them to take ownership of their ministry and to lean into their gifts as they serve.
5. **As you notice what volunteers do and don't like about serving, encourage them to lean into what they love.** If possible, eliminate responsibilities that they don't enjoy. Shift them into spaces that fit their gifts and passions.
6. **Let your volunteers have a voice in the ministry.** They can lend their perspective and their gifts to the ministry in broader ways and help you improve the ministry overall, not just in ways specific to their role.
7. **Encourage volunteers to take ownership of their ministry.** Some means that have worked for student ministry leaders include:
    - **Building buy-in and vision**
        - Give them purpose and remind them of the eternal impact they are having.

    - Point them back to Biblical truths like John 16:13 and Ephesians 4:11-12, helping them to see that ministry is not just the work of "professionals."
    - Give them a vision for the year by using an illustration.
    - Help volunteers see how their gifts help fulfill the ministry vision.
    - Longevity and ownership can often go hand-in-hand. Encourage them to commit long enough that they will get a taste of the long-term joy and impact.
    - Encourage volunteers to come on overnight trips to build deeper relationships with students, which can lead to more buy-in from the volunteers and stronger relationships with students.
  - **Creating opportunities for leadership**
    - Give them opportunities to lead things they are interested in, such as a game night they lead while you take a support role.
    - Notice where and how they are excited to serve, and then make sure they have the opportunity and resources to be able to succeed there.
  - **Empowering through trust and autonomy**
    - Delegate to empower your volunteers, rather than to keep them busy.
    - Don't micromanage your volunteers.
    - Take their ideas seriously.

        - Remind them to not try to be you, but to be themselves with students.
    - **Affirming and encouraging**
        - When you notice them taking ownership or using their gifts in creative ways, affirm and encourage them.
        - Encourage them to be praying about how God wants to use them, and to be obedient to how he is directing them through both prayer and the things others are affirming/seeing in them.

Encouraging Longevity

Longevity in volunteer leaders can have massive benefits for your ministry and your students. Longevity means that leaders can build relationships and increase their impact on students over the course of years with the same students, which can be incredibly powerful for discipleship. But longevity doesn't just happen on its own. Good stewardship of your volunteers can help promote longevity.

Therefore, you should have longevity and retention in mind as you manage your volunteers. In a sense, you are to play the long-game with them. Perhaps this is something you know how to do with students, but you've never thought about it when it comes to your volunteers.

Matthew McNutt, a long-time youth pastor, wrote his D.Min. dissertation on factors that influence longevity in student ministry volunteers. His research led him to conclude that **1) clarity in casting vision, communicating expectations, and clearly defined wins, 2) training volunteers, 3) strong relational connections with and amongst volunteers, 4) meaningful**

service, 5) rest, and 6) regular expression of appreciation were important factors that contribute to longevity.[1] As you look at that list, what stands out as something you could work on?

We've already discussed some of the factors that McNutt identified in other sections. However, you might want to additionally consider the following ideas to help you **encourage volunteer longevity**:

1. **Notice any factors that have helped promote longevity for volunteers so far, and continue to be intentional about those factors.** Ask some of your longest-tenured volunteers what has encouraged them to stick around to get some ideas.
2. **Don't overload or overuse your volunteers.** Be proactive to prevent burnout and invest in their need for rest. Some ways you might do that include:
   - Build in natural breaks for your volunteers. There should be some lulls in the calendar when they have time to step away and recharge.
   - Provide co-leaders for your volunteers. In doing so, no one volunteer is carrying a load by themselves. This also provides students consistency even when one volunteer has to miss.
   - After an overnight event or trip, consider giving volunteers the rest of the week off from their duties.

---

1. Matthew McNutt, "Exploring Factors Influencing Long-Term Volunteer Engagement and Retention in Student Ministry," Palmer Theological Seminary, 2025.

- If you're not sure what's too much for your volunteers, ask them.
- Look for ways to care for your volunteers in the midst of their roles. For example, provide a coffee and snack station for volunteers during an event or retreat.

3. **Have a well-defined plan for ongoing management of your volunteers, which includes things like training and clear communication with them.** This helps the leaders know what to expect and gives them a consistent, predictable experience, which can minimize frustrations.
4. **Maintain and rely on your relational connections with your volunteers.**
   - Create a sense of belonging and purpose for your volunteers. These sorts of things can be the glue that keeps a team together even in hard seasons.
   - Pay attention to your people, not just the processes you have in place. Having processes such as onboarding and training is necessary but not enough on its own. Your volunteers are people who will benefit from you noticing their needs. Know what's going on in their lives, and don't solely view them as someone filling a role.
   - Schedule one on ones with volunteers to maintain connection with them, address their concerns, and identify growth opportunities for them. Through these conversations, you can identify issues before they become big enough that a volunteer might want to exit.

5. **Help your volunteers see the impact of their ministry**, even in seasons when it feels like there's no fruit. Remind them also of the power of sticking with students for the long haul.
6. **Define for your volunteers what some clear "wins" are.** These help them recognize that when they have done their job and that they are needed. Without defining these for them, they may falsely think that they've only achieved a win when every kid in their small group is passionately following Jesus; as a result, they may become discouraged and think they're not up for the task when this doesn't happen. Defining "wins" for them upfront prevents these situations and helps them celebrate smaller wins along the way, minimizing discouragement and promoting longevity.
7. **Conduct exit interviews with volunteers when they step down from serving in the student ministry.** Use these interviews to gain feedback on what went well and what could be improved.

7

Honoring Volunteers

We have so many reasons to be grateful for volunteers. Ministry depends on volunteers. Therefore, **we ought to be intentional in honoring and thanking our volunteers**. Don't just assume they know how much you and others appreciate them – make a point to let them know they are highly valued! There are a lot of ways to do this, and you can also get creative with it. Be sure to plan around your budget and to match appreciation to your volunteers' personality and preferences. Here are some ideas you might use:

1. **Personal recognition and public acknowledgement**
    - Frequently encourage your volunteers. Tell them what you have noticed them doing well, or anything that someone else has shared about their impact.
    - Frequently sing their praises to others, such as church staff and elders.
    - Thank your volunteers any time they give up vacation or off time from work to go on trips with students. That's a huge sacrifice. You probably get some off time after a trip to recoup, but they are likely going right back to work on Monday morning.
    - Give volunteers opportunities to share stories of how they've seen God at work in their ministry or through another volunteer's ministry.

- Start a series in your newsletter or social media channels where you highlight one volunteer at a time.
- Create a bulletin board in your student ministry space where you highlight all of your volunteers. Maybe even leave out materials for your students to write encouraging notes and add them to the board.
- Send your volunteers encouraging handwritten notes and cards – for their birthday, for Christmas, for anytime you're particularly encouraged by them, or just because! Highlight things you've noticed them doing well or that you appreciate about them.
- Look for special ways to honor long-term volunteers for their faithfulness over years.

2. **Events and gatherings**
    - Host an event where you honor and celebrate your volunteers. Go above and beyond in some aspects of this event in whatever ways you can. Maybe you cook steaks, have some great desserts, or put extra time into making the event feel special. You could even hand out fun trophies to recognize the volunteers.
    - Have a once-a-year retreat for your volunteers which includes fun things that adults would like to do.
    - Throw a party or gathering for your volunteers. Maybe let them bring along their spouses. Make it a night focused merely on celebration and relationship, not on training or student ministry.

You could even make it more personable by hosting it in your own home.

- Have your students help plan a party for your volunteers.
- Create a regular consistency for these gatherings that are focused on honoring and treating your volunteers. Find a frequency that works well for your context and stick to it.

3. **Giving gifts to your volunteers**
    - Consider doing this at particular intervals (such as at the end of each semester) and after particular events (like an overnight trip).
    - Gift cards with a fun or personalized note are a great option.
    - Make customized gifts. Have your volunteers fill out a form that lets you know about things they like. Use these to make a gift basket or to give smaller gifts throughout the year.
    - If possible, spoil them. Maybe someone in your church has connections to a company where you can buy nice things or get services at a discount.
    - Give them youth group merchandise - like a baseball hat, good quality sweatshirt, or tumbler with the student ministry logo. Bonus: It can also increase their feelings of being part of the team.
    - If you don't have much budget for gifts, ask parents if they would like to contribute in some way to being able to appreciate the volunteers.
    - Ask students, parents, and/or elders to write letters of appreciation to the volunteers.

- Treat them every now and then with donuts and coffee or another simple treat waiting for them when they show up for their volunteering role.
- When you meet with your volunteers for check-ins, treat them to lunch or coffee.
- Consider gifts that will feed them spiritually and holistically, such as books, retreats, or time away.

8
Handling Issues With Volunteers

It's not a matter of *if* but *when* you will have to work through issues related to your volunteers. Don't be surprised when this happens – volunteers are human beings full of sin and weaknesses, and they're usually juggling many other responsibilities on top of being your volunteer. **Decide ahead of time what your general perspective on and approach to handling issues with volunteers will be so that you won't be caught off guard and become reactive. Putting some thought behind this will help you to be more responsive and intentional.**

A good plan for addressing issues with volunteers might include the following:

1. **Relational intelligence**
    - Make sure you are building relationships with your volunteers, so that you **have the relational capital with them that is necessary for hard conversations** with them.
    - **Take a curious posture toward the volunteer's problematic behavior.** Don't assume you know what's causing it. Instead, ask questions out of genuine curiosity, and you will be able to coach them more effectively as a result.
    - **Be aware of your weaknesses.** Maybe there's a hard conversation you need to have, but you're

hesitant or not sure how to go about it. Identify what's holding you back, and then tackle it. If you lack confidence – what would help you gain confidence for the decision or conversation? If emotions are holding you back – what emotions are they, and how can you give those to God?

2. **Knowing when and how to address issues**
    - **Not every issue needs to be addressed. But when an issue is important or persistent enough, don't let it slide.** Be the leader and address the issue. The volunteer may not even realize it's an issue if you don't address it.
    - **Point back to the agreed upon expectations and hold your leaders to those** (this is part of why it's so helpful to have written job descriptions for volunteers!).
    - **Some issues, if not resolved, are deal-breakers, and others aren't.** Know when an issue crosses this line for your ministry, because this will change how you handle it. For example, maybe you have a volunteer who is in a difficult season of life and has therefore become less available. In some cases, you may give them grace in your expectations for attendance for a season, and in other cases, you may ask them to step back for a season while someone else takes their spot.
3. **Planning for the conversation**
    - Think through what you want to make sure you communicate beforehand.
    - Consider Scripture that speaks into your approach, such as Matthew 18:15-17 and Ephesians 4:29-32.

- Preface or sandwich any correction with encouragement.
- Take a posture of, "I love how you're contributing to the ministry, and I want to help you get even better at that."
- You could say something like, "I really appreciate your presence on Wednesday nights and the way you ____________. I've also noticed that it seems you're having difficulty with ____________. I'd love to help you get better at that. Can you tell me what's going on there?"
- Some issues will take time to resolve, especially if they require a volunteer to grow in skills or maturity. Be prepared to keep coaching them throughout the process.

4. **Making hard decisions in the process**
   - **Repeated issues with one volunteer may indicate that they are not a good fit for volunteering with the student ministry.** Be willing to evaluate this honestly. Know the difference between "We've got the right person, and they just need help growing," and "While there are positives to the person, they just aren't the right person for this role." In the first case, you can approach issues with the posture of being committed to the leader and helping them grow; in the second, you need to release them from serving in the student ministry.
   - **Rely on the Holy Spirit's guidance.** Balancing correction and grace requires wisdom, and that doesn't look the same in every situation. Ask for

wisdom from the Spirit, and he will give it to you!

  - **With some issues, you should loop in a supervisor or other church leadership or ask for their input on the issue.** If you're not sure whether a situation calls for this, ask your supervisor for clarity on what kinds of volunteer issues they want to be in the loop on and which ones they would encourage you to handle on your own.

5. **Releasing volunteers when necessary**
   - It can be hard to tell someone they aren't a good fit for working with the student ministry, whether that's as they're applying to serve, 2 weeks in, or 8 years in. However, keep in mind that **both the student ministry and the leader will benefit from this decision**, even though it may feel hard at the moment.
   - **As much as you can, help them find another place to serve that may better fit their gifts.** You've likely made observations about what they are and aren't gifted in, and communicating these things to them in a gracious way can help them see more clearly how God has uniquely designed them and where they can best serve. This is how we discover how to best use our gifts in the body of Christ – by trying things out and getting honest feedback from others in the body!
   - With this in mind, you can steer the conversation such that they will be less likely to hear, "You aren't gifted," "You're no good," or "I don't like you,"

and more likely to hear, "You are gifted, and I think your gifts mean you should shift to __________." **Let them know that you want them to thrive in their giftings and service.**

The kinds of issues you will encounter with volunteers are many. Here are some common ones and ways you might approach them:

1. **A volunteer has become flaky or is consistently late.**
    - Ask the volunteer about their flakiness or tardiness. Get the story behind it, so you can respond appropriately.
    - If there's an extenuating circumstance that contributes, let the leader know that you need communication from them when they have timing conflicts. This way, you will know ahead of time if they will be absent and can plan accordingly.
    - Reiterate time expectations and help them work toward the goal of meeting them.
    - If you're having issues with one or more volunteers canceling on you at the last minute, consider how you can better communicate with leaders on the front end when they commit to something. For example, if a leader drops out just before an event or trip, this could jeopardize your ability to have the ratio of leaders to students that you need and thus jeopardize the safety and feasibility of the whole event. Help them understand the stakes and how much you are relying on their commitment.

2. **A volunteer has taken the approach of being friends with students more than being a leader to students, leading to poor boundaries and some poor influence on students.**
    - Talk with this ministry leader about incarnational ministry, which enters into youth culture without conforming to it. Emphasize that students don't just need more friends – they need Godly adults to teach them how to become Godly adults.
    - Pay attention to the spiritual needs that might exist behind this issue and tend to them. Is the leader looking for the students to make them feel accepted or important, for example? If so, provide spiritual encouragement in this area.
    - Teach them about healthy boundaries, and emphasize that we can draw boundaries and have limits because God is the one who is at work in the lives of students.
    - Help them recognize that there are times to be in "play and goof off" mode (like at a fun event with students), and that other settings (such as Sunday school) call for more of a classroom atmosphere. Encourage them to match their behavior with the setting – playful during play time, and serious during class time.
3. **A volunteer isn't good at what you've asked them to do.**
    - Assess what the volunteer needs. Are they missing skills you can teach them? Do they need coaching and mentoring in an area? Or is the role they are in simply a mismatch for them, and you should help

them find another way to serve that is better matched to their strengths? Figure out what's behind the problem, and form a plan from there.

4. **There is conflict between you and a volunteer, or between volunteers.**
    - Know that conflict is not a bad thing, but is simply something that happens when you have multiple people on a team. Conflict provides an opportunity to learn how to work through hard things together.
    - Be the leader and have the hard conversation to work through the conflict.
    - Address conflict in person or over the phone, not over text.
5. **Multiple ministries in the church want the same people as volunteers, and it feels like you're all competing for the best people.**
    - Talk with the other ministry leaders at your church. Get on the same page that you all want every ministry to thrive and you all want what's best for the volunteers. Work together toward solutions from that page, so that it feels like you're working on the same team, not against each other.
    - Allow the volunteers to have agency in the decisions of which ministries get them.
6. **A volunteer is giving up their own spiritual health or community (skipping church or involvement in an adult small group, for example) in order to be involved with student ministry.**
    - Re-emphasize the importance of personal soul care to this leader.

   - If needed, require them to step back to tend to their own spiritual health until they have more time open in their schedule for both their own spiritual needs and serving in the student ministry.
7. **You have lots of volunteer turnover.**
   - Assess how sustainable your expectations on leaders are over the long term.
   - Look for patterns. Are there any common "backdoors" that volunteers are exiting through?
   - Ask previous volunteers for feedback on why they left, and give them permission to be candid with you.
8. **You have too many volunteers.**
   - This can be both a great problem to have and an awkward problem to have. Maybe you asked too many people to be volunteers this year, or your youth group attendance shrunk and now the ratio of adults to students feels strange. Notice how this issue arose and what dynamics it's affecting.
   - Empower your volunteers to connect with students who aren't coming to youth group, in an effort to both disciple those students and to encourage them to attend youth group activities.
   - Consider dividing and conquering more roles for your volunteers at youth group.
   - Use the extra manpower to decrease everyone's load. Maybe you can now give everyone a co-leader, or give your volunteers permission to take a couple weeks off throughout the semester (as long as these are scheduled in a way so that you still have enough coverage every week!).

9

Ensuring Safety

To minister responsibly to minors, you must address safety. Our first priority is always to keep teenagers physically safe and to take seriously the fact that their parents have entrusted them to our care and supervision. There are at least two big factors that make this especially important for working with teens. First, teenage brains aren't yet fully developed, especially in the region that contributes to rational decision-making and awareness of risk and long-term consequences. Second, as minors, they are vulnerable to being taken advantage of by adults. For these reasons, we need leaders who act like responsible adults and will not abuse their power.

Any time you bring a new volunteer into the ministry, you are inherently taking a risk as you give this person church-endorsed access to minors. **Take that responsibility seriously.** A thorough safety plan related to your volunteers may include the following:

1. **Know your church's safety policies.** If your church doesn't have policies related to working with minors, work toward formulating one. Some good resources for this include Ministry Safe, Protect My Ministry, and *On Guard: Preventing and Responding to Child Abuse at Church* by Deepak Reju.
2. **Always screen your volunteers.** This is essential in order to create and maintain a safe environment.
3. **Make sure your volunteers know your policies and your procedures for safety issues.** Consider even

topics like appropriate physical contact, driving students in your car, first aid, medications, and active shooter/threat procedures.

4. **Train your volunteers in child abuse awareness and protection.** Also be sure to let them know what your state's laws are and whether they are a mandatory reporter.
5. **Train your volunteers in handling sensitive information and topics,** such as what to do if a student shares that they are (or another student is) in danger, harming themselves, or doing something illegal.
6. **If you notice a volunteer creating a potential safety issue, treat this as a matter of importance and urgency.** Don't delay in addressing it.
7. **Connect your volunteers with parents of students and create transparency about who is involved with students.** This could mean intentionally introducing volunteers and parents in church settings, including their names and/or pictures in an email to parents or on your website, or planning an open hang for parents and volunteers at a local coffee shop.

10
Considerations for Two Types of Volunteers

There are two kinds of people who can make great volunteers, but having them as volunteers also comes with extra dynamics to consider. These two kinds of people are parents of students and students themselves – let's look at both of these in turn.

Parents

Maybe you have a great volunteer team, but you have little to no parents on it. Why would you want to have parents as volunteers? Isn't youth group about letting students have their own space in the church, apart from their families? What value can the parents add to the ministry? If these are your thoughts, consider a few things.

First, **remember that parents are called to disciple their children, and the church and student ministry partner with them in this endeavor.** Part of your job description may even entail equipping parents to disciple their teenage children. A covenantal model of ministry leads student ministries to build bridges with parents, and between parents and students, rather than ignoring or shunning parents away from the ministry. This goes back to your philosophy of ministry – do you believe in the importance of parents discipling their children and of partnering with parents? If so, how are you practically implementing that into your ministry? **One way you can do that is through involving parents in your ministry as volunteers.**

Second, **consider the benefits of having parents as volunteers**. As parents become involved in the ministry, your relationships with parents will grow, and their understanding of and buy-in to the student ministry will grow. This is a great way to build trust with parents. Moreover, parents may have many qualities that it would be great to have in volunteers – such as maturity, parental instincts in emergencies or danger, and familiarity with the teenagers in your student ministry.

At the same time, you should be cautious about how you involve parents. One situation you probably want to avoid is having a parent be the small group leader for their own child. This can create negative dynamics for the child and other students, even if they are subtle. For instance, a parent may unintentionally show favoritism toward their child in the small group, and the other students may pick up on this and feel understandably slighted. The weaknesses that exist in the parent-child relationship at home would also carry over into the small group setting – whereas, if the student had a different small group leader, that leader might actually excel where the parent has a weakness. If they feel another adult is a better listener, for example, they may be willing to be more vulnerable with them than with their own parent (plus, with their own parent, they may also worry about getting into trouble if they share the wrong thing!).

Even if a parent isn't their own child's small group leader, many parents and students may feel uncomfortable with the dynamics created by having their parent/child in close proximity in student ministry settings. Maybe the student feels embarrassed by having their parent around, or the parent is aware that they have a hard time turning off "parent mode" when they notice their child's problematic behavior during youth group.

Students are in a stage of development where they are growing in independence as they prepare to be adults. This is a good thing, and it does require them to have space from their parents. In this stage, they also need adult influence outside of their parents. There will always be things in the student's life that their parents will miss or that they do not want to share with their parents, and other adults play a vital role in these areas. So, **for every student whose parent is a volunteer, make sure that other adults are also building relationships with that student.**

In light of these cautions, **take note of the dynamic of the family as you think about having particular parents as volunteers.** What is the parent-child relationship like? How do both the parent and the student feel about the parent getting involved as a volunteer – apprehensive, excited, or somewhere in between? With some student-parent dynamics, this will work pretty smoothly, and with others, it will be something you need to have open conversations about with both the student and the parent more often in order to navigate well.

Many student ministries have found parents to be great small group leaders, as long as they don't have the parent lead their own child's small group. However, **you may also want to consider putting a parent in a role other than a small group leader.** Maybe they can help with snacks, chaperone a mission trip, host an event at their home, or provide extra hands at a larger event. Parents also make great additions to student ministry advisory committees, as they provide input from real stakeholders in your ministry. When parents are involved in these ways, they can also use their relational capital with other families to draw them in and increase involvement and buy-in of others.

As you involve parents and ask for their input, however, **be aware that parents can be prone to view the ministry through the eyes of their child(ren) only**. That is, they may need to be reminded that their child's experience and preferences are not necessarily representative of the experience and preferences of all the students in the student ministry. If you can help them to take on a broader perspective, their voice and contributions will be even more valuable.

As you consider whether to recruit and accept parents as volunteers, keep in mind these dynamics, and **have an open conversation with the parent on the front end** about it. As parents serve in your ministry, pay attention to how their service is affecting their parent/child relationship. If issues arise there, do what you can do to address them and to use the opportunity to build a bridge between the student and parent. If improvement is unsatisfactory, however, consider moving the parent into a different role; the negative effects in the parent-child relationship are not worth it, because that relationship is of utmost importance for the student's wellbeing and faith development.

Finally, perhaps you would like more parents as volunteers but they are reluctant. **To recruit more parents, give them a vision and address their concerns.** Help them see why they'd make a good volunteer, and why you want parents as volunteers. Tell them stories (from other youth groups, if need be) about how parents have made great volunteers. Take them back to your vision and philosophy. Ask about their hesitancies, and tell them how they can be involved in ways that aren't overbearing to their children.

Students

As you minister to students, **an important question to ask yourself is how you will equip students to minister to and disciple others themselves.** Many churches let students contribute to service projects or lead within nursery and children's ministry, but as a student matures, you can also invite them to serve within the student ministry.

Student volunteers are an incredibly valuable addition to student ministry. **As a student contributes to the ministry, they grow in leadership, in their involvement and buy-in to the ministry, and in their relationship with you as the leader.** You may notice that the relationships and conversations you have with student leaders become particularly sweet and fruitful, as they become partners in ministry with you. As you train and coach them, you are discipling them and helping them develop their gifts for kingdom service. Even when issues come up – and they will, since students will be the youngest and least mature volunteers you have – these are opportunities to further disciple them.

There are many approaches you could take to involving students as leaders within your ministry. Some student ministries have a robust student leadership program which equips high school students to minister to middle school students through helping lead small groups, engaging in relational ministry, and even serving as additional leaders for trips and events. In these settings, the high school students are generally serving alongside adult volunteers. Another model might use students in different roles – such as serving on a music or tech team, leading games, teaching youth group lessons, or leading prayer. In this model, both middle and high school students could conceivably be offered opportunities to serve, and students would be funneled to roles that fit their giftings and passions. These are but two models, and you should decide what would work best for your context.

As with parent volunteers, student volunteers also require student ministry leaders to be thoughtful about potential backfalls and complications.

Just like with parent volunteers, **family dynamics can be a factor you need to consider – but in this case, it's the often tricky dynamics between siblings.** For instance, when a student is given leadership and their sibling is also in the youth group, you may notice that sibling B may not be receptive to sibling A's leadership. Just as putting a parent in charge of their child's small group is usually not the best choice, letting a high schooler lead their own younger sibling's small group is often not advisable. Therefore, you may want to have a conversation with potential student leaders on the front end about the potential pitfalls they could find themselves in as their sibling relationship impacts their leadership and vice versa.

You will also need to be prepared to navigate issues carefully with student volunteers in order to maintain a good relationship with them. It is possible that you will have to "fire" them as a volunteer at some point, and you will want to do this gracefully, in order to not discourage them from continuing to be involved in the ministry as a student.

Pay attention to how your policies inform how students can serve as leaders. Does your policy require a certain ratio of students to adults? Remember that students under 18 do not count as adults, so while they are leaders, they will not help you get to the necessary ratio. You may also need to consider what other requirements – such as background checks and sexual abuse awareness training – might apply or not apply to minors serving as leaders.

Be sure to have a good application and interview process for student volunteers. This will help you to turn away students who want to lead but are not ready, and to do this in a way that avoids the appearance of outright favoritism. It's also helpful to have the parents involved in some way in this process, such as having them sign the application and an agreement that verifies they understand what the student is committing to. You will also need their permission if you have to run a background check, and you should inform them if you will be training the student leaders in any sensitive topics.

Finally, you might want to train student volunteers separately from your adult leaders. This allows you to tailor student volunteer training to their needs, which may be distinct enough from the needs of your adult volunteers to warrant separate trainings. Additionally, it allows your adult volunteers space to discuss questions and concerns that it might be best to not have teens around for. For example, adult volunteers have discussed prayer requests and concerns about high school students in the presence of high school student volunteers at our volunteer training. This put students in the uncomfortable position of hearing adults talk about their peers, which also didn't protect the privacy of their peers.

Conclusion

Working with volunteers in student ministry is difficult – but it is also a central part of student ministry, not a peripheral task. As ministry leaders, we are called to equip the saints for the work of ministry. Student ministry is the work of the body of Christ, and that means that getting volunteers involved from your church isn't just about having enough people to meet your required student to adult ratios – it's about the church functioning as God designed it.

Your head may be spinning with ideas from this book, and you may not be sure where to start. **Remember, this book is not intended to be a plan that you fully implement; it's meant to be a collection of ideas that you can draw from. So, pick somewhere to start.** Maybe you've always struggled with having enough volunteers, and you need to key in first on improving your recruitment strategies. Or maybe you've got a good team, but you're seeing the need for better training or leadership on your end.

Pick a couple priorities, and start there. Don't try to implement a hundred new things at once. **What's one or two things you can implement in the next 30 days?**

As you invest in your volunteer ministry, the fruit may seem slow – but trust that it's worth it. Investing in volunteers multiplies your student ministry's long term impact, and it develops the volunteers for further kingdom impact, no matter how long they volunteer with the ministry. Remember that God is at work, even when it seems like he's not – not only in students' lives, but also in your volunteers' lives.

Sample Forms & Documents for Volunteers

For sample forms and documents you can use with your volunteers, visit https://rym.org/resources-ministry-tool-downloads

About RYM

Reformed Youth Ministries exists to serve the Church in its efforts to reach and equip youth for Christ. Through its primary avenues of ministry: **conferences, training** and **resources;** everything RYM does is oriented to help churches as they seek to raise up the next generation of the Church with the Gospel of Jesus Christ.

reformed youth ministries

www.rym.org

Made in the USA
Coppell, TX
17 June 2026

81289911R00056